PLAYFUL PRESCHOOL PIANO TEACHING

Nicola Cantan

NICOLA CANTAN is a piano teacher, author, blogger and creator of imaginative and engaging teaching resources from Dublin, Ireland. She loves getting piano students learning through laughter and exploring the diverse world of music making through improvisation, composition and games.

Nicola's membership site, *Vibrant Music Teaching*, is helping teachers all over the world to include more games and off-bench activities in their lessons, so that their students giggle their way through music theory and make faster progress.

Nicola also runs a popular blog, *Colourful Keys*, where she shares creative ideas and teaching strategies, and hosts regular training events for piano teachers.

PLAYFUL PRESCHOOL PIANO TEACHING

Nicola Cantan

Colourful Keys Books

Published in the Republic of Ireland

First Printing, 2019

ISBN 978-1-913000-13-4

Colourful Keys
78 Durrow Road
Dublin, D12 V3A3

www.vibrantmusicteaching.com

To tiny little musicians all over the world.

CONTENTS

STARTING

"You will never win if you never begin."
Helen Rowland

My first three preschool piano students could not have been more different. The very first was the daughter of a Montessori teacher. She was remarkably focused, followed every direction, grasped every concept with ease and had great finger dexterity for her age.

Talk about a false sense of security.

The next student was a rude awakening. He did not seem to understand any of the activities I had planned, wouldn't stay on task, and couldn't really use a crayon, let alone play piano keys with each of his fingers individually.

The third was very bright, well behaved and capable... but (to put it mildly) did *not* take a shine to me. He didn't want to do what I wanted him to do, even though he could.

Of course, I learnt the most from the second two students. The second student inspired some of my earliest piano teaching games which I began to share on my blog, *Colourful Keys*. He taught me to break down concepts into smaller parts than I knew existed and gave me insights into teaching techniques that I could use with students of all ages. The third taught me a simple but vital lesson about relationships which we'll discuss in the 'Copying' chapter.

STARTING WITH A DIVERSE VIEW

I'm the youngest of five siblings, and my mother says that each time she had a child she expected them to be similar to one of her other children. When she had her second child she was astonished that he was nothing like the first. The third was completely different to the first two, and the fourth was yet again unique. (The fifth was me, of course, and since I'm the only girl I think she was expecting something different that time.) My mum is being a bit tongue-in-cheek when she explains this. But her point is that, even within the same family, with one pool of genes, it is pretty amazing that children can be so different in temperament, personality, likes and dislikes.

If you tried to teach the same piano lesson in exactly the same way to each one of us at age four you would have a mess on your hands. There would be leg jiggling and wriggling from some and overwhelm from others. Some lessons would be pure chaos and others would be sluggish to the point of sleepiness. Chances are not one of these lessons would be what you could consider "successful" unless you got very lucky.

When I set out to write this book I wanted to represent as wide a sample of 3–5-year-old children and their teachers as I could, knowing, as my mother discovered, that there is an infinite number of "types" of people.

That's why as part of my research I reached out to three wonderful preschool piano teachers from three different continents to discuss their experiences of teaching tiny fingers to play piano. You'll find their ideas and quotes from our conversations throughout the book, so let me introduce you to them here before we get started.

Lyndel Kennedy

Lyndel Kennedy lives in Perth, Australia with her husband and their four children. She believes in a world where everyone is created to be musical.

Her programs have emerged from her rich music and visual arts career spanning graphic design, videography, photography, storytelling, and over 30 years of piano teaching. Her musical journey began as a young child, and included opportunities to play at national level competitions through to directing school musicals and choirs, attending Composition Master Classes with conductor and screen composer Brian May, and conducting international teacher workshops. Lyndel is passionate about encouraging students and teachers, wherever they are on the journey, to express their own musical identity.

Kris Skaletski

Kris Skaletski is the creator and publisher of KiddyKeys® piano and Music All-Star teaching materials. She has over 35 years of experience leading piano lesson programs and preschool music, teaching in both home and school settings in Green Bay, Wisconsin. In 2015, Kris partnered up with Jennifer Eklund of Piano Pronto® to co-author the Roadtrip!® piano books for young beginners. She has recently released Piano Playground and Under the "C" piano books for rote learning and note learning.

A lifelong Green Bay area resident, Kris and her husband, Jack, have two grown children. An avid Green Bay Packers fan, Kris also enjoys tending her flower beds and a morning cup of coffee on her front porch.

Carina Busch

Carina Busch runs her own piano studio from her home near Düsseldorf in Germany and teaches all ages, starting from four years. She loves to try new ideas and accompany her students on their way to a well-rounded knowledge of music and playing the piano.

Carina writes a blog about piano teaching and her ideas and experiences. Written in German, it can be found at: klavierpaedagogikentdecken.de ("discovering piano pedagogy").

Both Lyndel and Kris have their own programs for preschool piano, and I have two myself (one for private lessons, one for group lessons) inside my *Vibrant Music Teaching* membership. **But this book is not specific to any one of those methods or programs.** This book is about bringing together different thoughts, ideas and principles of preschool piano teaching so that you can do it *your* way. That's the beauty of it, and I'm so grateful to all three women for understanding that and being generous enough to share their experiences so that we can spread music to all five of my mum's different types of children, and beyond.

STARTING WITH PLAY

If you don't read a single word of the rest of this book (I hope you do, of course, but *if* you don't), I hope you will read and digest the 'Playing' chapter.

Play should be in everything you do with your preschool students. Play is how they understand the world, and including playfulness (and a bit of silliness too if you're up for it) is your surest route to success with your young students.

Whenever you feel the urge to ask your preschool piano student to "please concentrate, because this is important!" I want you to instead *ask yourself* whether they're **having fun and exploring music.** If the answer is yes, they are learning – just maybe not in the way you expected them to. And rather than trying to control their pathway to learning we should focus on controlling our urge to control. We'll talk more about effective play-based teaching strategies in the 'Playing' chapter.

STARTING TO "ING"

As you scan the Contents page of this book, you may notice something a little unusual. Every chapter title ends with an "–ing". I've chosen these active words because that's what preschool piano teaching should be: active. We need to keep things moving to teach these little ones effectively, and this book will guide you through how to do that in three important stages.

In Part 1 we'll focus on getting ready to teach preschool students. This includes making decisions about your lesson format, equipment and fees. But we'll also look at getting into the right mindset for teaching these wee ones by putting aside your preconceptions about what piano lessons should look like so that you can start with a clean slate.

The largest section of the book, Part 2, is devoted to the specific things you and your preschool students will be doing in your piano lessons: playing, sitting, moving, seeing, copying, reading, singing, listening and creating. Because I wanted this book to be stupendously practical, in these chapters you will find not only guidelines but specific examples that will help you apply these teaching activities and strategies in your own lessons.

In Part 3 we'll look at what happens outside of your

preschool lessons to make them successful: home practice, performances and the planning you need to do to fit all the activities together.

I have also put the focus in this book firmly on the "–ing" because I really want you to get out there and *do*. This book is not a philosophical exploration of the best ways to teach piano to preschoolers in theory. None of these ideas mean anything if you don't put them into practice. You don't need to try them all out at once, but you do need to try them. If many of these ways of teaching are new to you, just try one new thing at a time. Then, when you're ready, come back and pick out another one to try.

I hope that at the end of this book you will feel confident and well equipped to go into your preschool piano lessons, give new ideas a go, and find out what works for you and your students.

PART 1
Before lessons begin

I found my very first student by posting flyers through doors when I was 15 years old. I charged €8 for lessons in my parents' house and €2 extra for lessons at the student's home. Of course, with those rates all of the families opted for lessons in their home, so for years I cycled 20–30 minutes each way for less than the cost of a coffee.

Over the years, I made plenty of other mistakes in my business as I gradually learnt to treat it *as a business.*

Whether you're just getting started, or have been teaching for years but have just not branched out into preschool lessons yet, it's worth taking a bird's-eye view first. In this section, we'll look at the big picture of teaching preschool students before zooming into the details. We'll go through each of the decisions you need to make so that you don't end up like my teenage self working for four bucks an hour (or something equally poorly planned).

Chapter 1
DECIDING

"Nothing happens until you decide. Make a decision and watch your life move forward."
Oprah Winfrey

The first thing we're going to tackle is all those decisions that need to be made to run successful preschool piano lessons. I know that the business side of your piano studio is probably not your favourite part, which is why we're going to eat our metaphorical veggies first and get it sorted right off the bat. If you would prefer to skip ahead to the fun stuff (the teaching strategies and activities) and come back to this later, then go for it. But do make sure to come back to this chapter.

Fun is a serious business: you can't have fun if you don't take your business seriously. This chapter will help you think through the logistics and the money, so that your head is not buzzing with numbers and policies and you can focus on teaching and actually enjoying your lessons.

In this section we'll go through all the major decisions you will need to make before any tiny feet even set foot in your studio. Consider each area in this section carefully. Imagine yourself teaching the types of classes described and see what feels right for you. Every teacher is different and there is no one right answer, so take your time when making these decisions.

But don't take too long. It can be tempting to keep collecting ideas, thinking and brainstorming as a way to avoid starting something new and scary. Because if you start you might fail...right? Trust me: at some point you just need to dive in. Fake it till you make it, be brave, and don't get caught in analysis paralysis.

DECIDING BETWEEN PRIVATE AND GROUP

The first decision you should make is whether you'll teach in groups or one-on-one. For most piano teachers, private lessons feel more familiar and it seems like less of a leap to teach these tiny fingers in our regular lesson format. However, if you try to teach preschoolers in the same way you teach older students, you're going to run aground pretty quickly, so bear in mind that it won't really be "regular" anyway. We'll deal with this more in the 'Forgetting' chapter, but it's a very rare preschooler who will be able to focus for 30 minutes of sitting at the piano following black and white dots across lines on a page.

So this decision should not be made based on your comfort zone, because you're going to have to go off-road anyway. There are three important factors to weigh up when considering group and one-on-one lessons for preschoolers:

- Profit
- Progress
- Planning

There's only so much you can charge a parent for your time. If you teach more than one student at a time, your money making potential will go up. We'll talk more about actual fee calculations later in this chapter, but profitability is something to bear in mind. How important this factor is to you will depend on your circumstances and on how easily you can envisage yourself teaching a group of 3–8 ~~hyperactive scamps~~ *precious little angels.*

If you're torn on the profitability factor, spend some time working out the actual difference in take-home pay. For this you will need to know the minimum number of students you would have in your group and whether you would need to pay additional expenses, such as rent, for example, to run your classes. Plan out each lesson option as you work through the sections below and make the decision when you've thoroughly considered all avenues.

I run both group and solo lessons for preschoolers in my studio, and when parents are weighing up the options I frame it in terms of progress versus parent participation. (We could debate what progress means all day long...for now let's take it to mean being able to play songs/pieces on the piano.) Group classes will usually make slower progress than one-on-one lessons, but they are more social and, for many kids and their parents, a great low-pressure first introduction to music and the piano. In fact, in my studio I don't require any practice from students in my *Mini Musicians* group classes, so progress is definitely slower-paced. For now just keep in mind that, if your prospective piano parents are looking to "get ahead" or have competitive ambitions for their preschool pianist, private lessons are probably going to be the best fit. If, however, they're looking for an enriching musical experience without a serious commitment on their part, group lessons are perfect.

The progress your students make in either lesson format, however, will be closely tied to the parents' involvement at home (we'll talk more about how to get parents involved in the 'Practising' chapter).

The last factor to consider in this decision is the lesson planning. If you are going to teach any type of preschool lesson, or any unfamiliar type of lesson for that matter, it is going to take more planning initially. For private lessons, you may be able to do this planning yourself using a solid method book and a bit of online investigation. For group lessons, you will most likely need to invest in a program. Planning out group lessons yourself or trying to "wing it" each week is going to lead to frustration and a sharp nose-dive in your profitability. Unless you plan to sell your curriculum to other teachers later on, the time you invest in putting it together will mean that you make a pitiful effective hourly rate[1] for your group preschool classes.

If you're looking to save on this planning time, I have a curriculum for group preschool lessons, *Mini*

---

1 Your effective hourly rate is the amount you actually make per hour for your teaching time once you have accounted for your costs and the admin and planning time you put into each lesson.

Musicians, and one for solo lessons, *Tiny Finger Takeoff*, inside my *Vibrant Music Teaching* membership. Whether you choose one of these curricula or another established program, make sure you have a plan for your lessons that is cost-effective and that you account for any additional licensing or membership fees.

Kris and Lyndel have taught preschoolers in both group and private lessons, and they prefer group lessons for most students. Kris loves how the students learn from each other in a group and likes to mix up the ages to get the full benefit.

"Personally, I still land in the group department because I really like the social interaction of a group, and I like mixed age groups – putting two-and-a-half- or three-year-olds with a four- or five-year-old in a lesson – because I think that they can be encouraged to model what we would do in our day-to-day lives. If we're with a group of piano teachers we don't put all of the 30-year-old teachers together and all the 35-year-old teachers together. We're positive peer mentors for each other. I can do everything I would do in a private piano lesson but the students get the social structure of a group."

Lyndel always has parents in her group lessons with the kids, and she gets everyone involved. She finds that everyone feeds off one another and this buzz creates a great environment for her creative story-based classes that helps make sure everyone is engaged and learning all the time.

"What I love is that my energy level is off-the-page in a group. It's exciting. The kids are excited, the parents are laughing. There's this amazing energy that comes from multiple people contributing to the conversation. I love it because the responsibility isn't always on me to demonstrate ideas and take it to the next level, because I'm actually learning from my students. That's true in private lessons as well, but in a group we're all learning from each other and inputting ideas all the time. And kids of this young age are not inhibited like us adults. They're like: 'Oh my goodness I want to do that. That's so cool!' I just love that interactive energy that happens in a group."

DECIDING HOW LONG YOUR LESSONS SHOULD BE

Many teachers' initial instinct is to offer shorter lessons of just 15 or 20 minutes for preschoolers. After all, 3–5-year-olds don't have the attention span needed for a 30-minute lesson, do they? It may shock you to know that I could happily spend 45 minutes or even an hour working one-on-one with a preschool student. I think that once you have read this book, and have seen just how many different activities you can do with preschool students and how much they can learn, you'll feel the same way too.

Let's address this "attention span" issue. It's true: preschoolers cannot sit still and focus for a half-hour stretch. (By the way, neither can older students, and neither can you or I...not *really*. Not to our fullest potential.) But they have plenty of attention span.

Preschoolers are capable of focussing on and puzzling through something they find engaging, accessible and relevant. It's up to us to teach them the way they learn. It's our job to build in repetition and reinforcement of concepts, and to structure our lessons so that they feel confident and capable.

Right, right...so how long should the lessons be, then?

In my opinion, private preschool lessons should be a minimum of 30 minutes each week or, ideally, 45 minutes. For group lessons, 30 minutes is possible but will feel quite rushed and is best for no-practice gentle-progress style classes. An hour is ideal for most groups, especially for those that involve the parents as well, and you'll be surprised how quickly it goes by. However, 45-minute group classes are definitely doable if this suits your goals and structure better.

For another perspective, Kris is happiest with 30-minute group lessons.

"Most of my teaching was done moving around from place to place, and if I was in a childcare centre or preschool I had to stick to a half-hour session. I also like them wanting more when they leave. I wanted them to be like 'oh, class is over?!' when they finished. Leave them on a high note of wanting more."

DECIDING WHAT EQUIPMENT YOU'LL NEED

If you decide to do private preschool piano lessons, and you're already a piano teacher, you probably have everything you need. Even for many group programs you may not need more than one instrument, as they're often structured so that children take turns at the piano. Some group programs will require a keyboard/piano for each child or for each pair of children, depending on the specific lesson plans and structure.

The choice of instrument (weighted or unweighted keyboard, acoustic piano, etc.) will be based upon your space, portability requirements (e.g. if you're teaching in daycare centres you may need to carry the instrument around) and your goals for your students. If you want them to work on playing with good technique straight away then you will need weighted keys.

No matter how many instruments you have or what type you choose, there are two things that will be essential:

- An adjustable bench that goes up to a height of about 60cm (24in)
- A footstool (preferably adjustable) that goes up to a height of about 26cm (10in)

You can certainly piece together this setup using carpet squares or towels on top of your non-adjustable bench and cheap footstools or plastic boxes at various heights. Just make sure that your student will be stable and at a good playing height with feet firmly planted when they're at the piano. We'll talk more about the ins and outs of this setup in the 'Moving' chapter.

There are other pieces of equipment used in many preschool curricula which are nice to have:

- Rhythm instruments, such as finger cymbals, drums, tambourines, maracas and egg shakers. I recommend buying an educational set from a reputable company. Safety and durability are extremely important when working with young children.
- Pitched percussion, such as deskbells, handbells, glockenspiels, chime bars and Boomwhackers. These are an excellent way to work on concepts that preschool students don't have the fine motor control to execute at the piano but do have the ability to understand.
- Floor mats or a small table with chairs for playing games, doing puzzles and colouring.
- Scarves or ribbon sticks for dancing and moving to music.
- A good sound system for playing music to march, tap and dance along to.

Please don't feel like you need to make a shopping list and go pick up all of these things right away! Start with a few things that you think you'll get the most use out of and go from there. You can build up your collection little by little over time.

DECIDING WHERE YOU'LL HOLD YOUR LESSONS

While you may be able to hold your preschool lessons or classes in the same space as your regular piano lessons, it may be useful to consider some alternative locations, depending on the type of lessons you wish to offer. Depending on your local area or community, 3–5-year-olds may have other commitments in the morning. Many are attending daycare, crèche, Montessori or kindergarten. To make the best use of the daytime hours, therefore, you may wish to approach these schools and childminding facilities to see if you can offer a program as part of their timetable. You may need to pay a fee or give a percentage of your fees to the company in order to offer this service, but it could be worth it. For many, one of the benefits of offering preschool lessons is that you can fill up these daytime hours, which will enable you to make more money or have more free time in the evenings...or both!

If you're considering this as an option, start by figuring out how much you would need to charge to cover your teaching time, admin, equipment and travel before approaching these companies in your area to see if they're interested. You can then negotiate to come up with a solution that will benefit you both.

DECIDING HOW MUCH YOU'LL CHARGE

Repeat after me: "Smaller fingers **do not** equal lower fees."

Got it? OK. I just wanted to make sure we got that out of the way up front. I don't know where this idea to charge preschool students less than your going rate came from. If it wouldn't have occurred to you to do so, don't give it another thought. If, however, you have been tempted to charge lower rates for your youngest students, consider these three facts:

- If anything, 3–5-year-olds require *more* energy to teach, not less
- As someone who provides a service, your time is your most precious commodity
- You are going to invest more time in planning and training in order to teach these little ones (heck, you're reading this book right now!)

So, if you're going to teach one-on-one preschool piano lessons and you're already teaching other students, the calculation is pretty simple. Just charge whatever you're already charging.

If this will be your first foray into group teaching, however, it will take some more consideration. The first decision to make in this case is the minimum number of students you will have in your class. What is the lowest number of students you would be willing to run the class with? Two? Five?

Once you know your minimum student numbers, you need to work out your minimum pay for the teaching time. I recommend at least two times your regular teaching rate (or more if your market will bear it). So if you charge $60 for a 45-minute private lesson you should aim to make at least $120 for a 45-minute group class. If the minimum number of students you will run the class with is three, then you will be charging each student $40 per class.

You need to make more for a group class than you would for a private lesson because there will likely still be the same admin time required for each student in the class and because you will spend more time planning and preparing for group classes than for private lessons. It's also best to base your calculations on the minimum number of students so that if you end up with a class that is not maxed out you will still feel good about teaching that class. You won't be scrambling to fill the class or feel resentful of the class time because you would prefer to simply have time off rather than teach for a pitiful fee. Plus, if you do fill the class to capacity the extra fees will feel like a bonus!

Some general fee notes:

A full discussion on setting fees and running an effective piano teaching business is beyond the scope of this book, but I want to briefly mention a few more things here – some general best practices for all piano teachers:

- Do not charge by the lesson
- Maintain studio policies
- Keep track of your expenses

The calculation I gave you above was based on a per-lesson rate, but I don't want you to think that I'm encouraging you to charge that fee at the door at each lesson. It is much more effective and sustainable to charge a flat monthly fee or on a semester/term basis. Paying by the lesson encourages people to think they can drop in and out of lessons when it suits them, and leads to a very unstable income for you.

A simple and succinct set of studio policies is a must for any piano teaching studio, even if you only have a few students or only teach a few hours a week. Remember how we need to take our business seriously in order to have fun? Studio policies are a great example of this. If you don't have guidelines which detail when you're paid, what happens if students miss a lesson, and other important details, you'll end up chasing your tail. You'll be too stressed to actually enjoy sharing music with your students because your mind will be whirring with whether suchand-such a family paid last month and what to do about the makeup lesson demands that you can't fit into your schedule. Do yourself, your students and their parents a favour and write a simple policy document. **And stick to it.**

Most teachers do not have a business degree and they can find keeping books intimidating. Many will simply pass off their receipts or records to an account-ant at tax time and dust their hands of it. While this may fulfill your legal obligations, it's not enough. You need to understand what's going on in your business so that you can make better decisions and adjust-ments when needed. Taking control of your accounts can be empowering and it doesn't need to be com-plicated. There are many low-cost or free accounting apps that will allow you to see where your expenses could be trimmed down and where there's scope for bringing in more income. Set up a simple system that works for you and make sure to check your numbers at least once a month. You'll sleep easier because of it.

Chapter 2
FORGETTING

"The beginning is always today."
Mary Shelley

Get ready to forget everything you know about piano teaching.

Well, not quite. But you will need to put aside many of your preconceptions about teaching and much of your experience as a teacher. Preschool lessons are a whole other game. Because 3–5-year-olds' brains are different to eight-year-olds' brains. It sounds obvious, but it's one of those things you need to keep coming back to when you find yourself confused by a pre-school student's reaction or frustrated by their lack of understanding.

Let's take a short detour into an alternate universe to a town called Grownupville.

Everything is enormous in Grownupville. All the trees tower above you like great redwoods, the stairs are about 30cm (1ft) high – almost twice the height of stairs in our universe – and the door handles are so high that you can only just reach them. In short, it's difficult to get around.

One day your boss in Grownupville tells you you're going to learn a new instrument, the toofpranie. She tells you you're going to go to a nice lady's house to learn how to play. You're not really sure what this is about but you trust your boss and she says it's going to be great. So off you go to your lesson.

The lesson is a pretty overwhelming experience. The toofpranie turns out to be an enormous instrument with a bewildering arrangement of keys that your teacher expects you to navigate.

The teacher points to one of the white keys (which are enormous – probably to fit her huge fingers) close to the middle of the toofpranie (but not quite in the centre) and announces that this is middle Γ (gamma). Then she points to a book she's placed in front of you and tells you that this is what middle Γ looks like on the flibbidy.

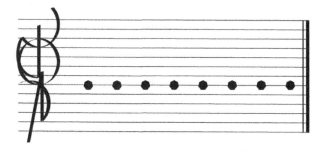

She asks you to play one middle Γ for every 'tean' you see. She points to the first one and looks at you expectantly...

But, as she says this, something catches your eye. You suddenly notice there are bright sparkling objects on the shelf above her toofpranie; they're almost flashing in the lights. You look around the room to see if there are any more and to try and figure out the source of the light...and then you hear a "tap-tap" sound.

Your teacher is tapping a pencil on the first tean, waiting for you to begin.

You're panicking. Where on earth was middle Γ again? The clock's ticks are practically deafening and it feels like you might get told off if you don't act soon, so you decide to just take a random stab, picking a white key roughly in the middle (but not quite) of the toofpranie. Your teacher looks at you quizzically, picks up your hand and puts it on a different key. She says: "This is middle Γ."

You're not sure how you're ever going to remember that but she seems like a nice lady so you're going to do your best to please her. You play through the song (if you can call it that – does this lady really like such dull music?) as she points to the teans. She seems satisfied and turns the page...

I haven't been a preschooler for quite some time and I don't think any of us can assume to really know what it's like inside the brain of a four-year-old. But I think this exercise can give us some insight into what it might feel like.

Yes, the patterns of black keys on the piano are a lot more decipherable to us than those on the toofpranie, but preschoolers are not as finely tuned to noticing such patterns as we adults are. And we may think that the Roman alphabet is easier than Greek, or that our musical words and symbols are easier to remember than those on the flibbidy, but if you've never heard any of them before then they're really not so simple, are they?

A big part of what you need to teach preschoolers, especially in the initial months, is how to see, navigate and understand patterns. They need to be able to filter out extraneous information and focus on what's relevant. Almost everything in your studio probably feels like the weird sparkling objects in our story. A 3–5-year-old hasn't got enough experience yet to be able to ignore all of the brand spanking new information contained within your teaching room and zero in on the staff. And not just on the staff, but on the note heads specifically, ignoring the stems until they're relevant.

This is why you need to completely forget what a standard piano lesson looks like when it comes to teaching preschoolers. Much of a standard lesson plan assumes that your student can see these patterns and filter out the irrelevant stuff without any conscious effort. That's not so with 3–5-year-olds. They're very much still learning to sort the world into categories, still creating their brain's filing system to manage the daily onslaught of new information.

Forget what a piano lesson *should* look like and focus on what the child sitting in front of you needs to know to take that next micro-step on their musical journey.

FORGETTING WHAT A LESSON "SHOULD" LOOK LIKE

Start with a blank slate. Throw out your expectations about what counts as a piano lesson or a general music class; the lines are much more blurred with preschoolers.

Once you've mentally cleared the decks, there are two approaches you can take to designing your preschool piano lessons, and I suggest you try out both of these to help you get your bearings.

Firstly, ask yourself what you expect a piano lesson to include. What are the basic elements you have in most of your lessons with older students? Make a list of these components. For example:

- Scales
- Reading pieces
- Theory worksheets

Now consider what each one is *for* so that you can start swapping them out for more developmentally appropriate options.

- Scales = technique or how we use our bodies
- Reading pieces = playing music

- Theory worksheets = developing musicianship and understanding

Do this as an exercise in stripping back a standard piano lesson to the fundamentals.

Now try the second approach: start from a completely blank slate. Knowing what you know at this stage, based on your experience teaching students of other ages, what activities could you do in your preschool lessons? If you had to teach a four-year-old tomorrow, without reading any further, what would you do? Write a list so you can see where you're starting from.

This isn't going to be your final lesson plan – you'll know more by the end of this book – but by discarding all your preconceptions in this way, you'll start thinking more proactively about what you put in your lessons.

Don't do anything because you "should". Always plan and teach with intention.

FORGETTING THE TYPICAL PROGRESS MARKERS

When the subject of teaching preschool piano lessons comes up in teaching groups, you'll often have a portion of teachers arguing that it's a waste of time. Their reasoning is normally that if a student starts at age five they'll be at the same point at age ten as they would be if they had started at age seven.

This may sometimes be true...if we only measure progress in terms of reading ability. So the question is whether "learning to play piano" is synonymous with "learning to read piano music". Is reading music, and playing it exactly as written, all we teach?

Gosh, I hope not. I hope we're at least teaching students rhythm skills, aural skills and theory that go beyond the notes on the page. And, on top of that, I believe we should also be teaching students to improvise, compose and play music by rote and by ear. The student who started at age five is going to be much further along in all these areas.

But there's one thing that those teachers are right about: progress will not look the same in preschool lessons as it does in lessons with older beginners. Reading progress especially will be slower-paced, as will most areas of technique. Three- to five-year-olds, however, will often develop just as quickly in their aural and rhythm work, and they will get a huge head start in these areas that will last a lifetime. Students who start music at a young age often develop far superior relative pitch than those that start even a few years later. Without knowing anything about their previous musical experience, I can usually spot in the very first lesson a student who has had early childhood music classes, or has learnt another instrument in school, by their pitch awareness and aural memory. And in these skills they stay ahead of their peers throughout their studies.

So you may need to ditch your ideas about how

quickly students should move through a method book and forget about how quickly you expect them to be able to identify note names six months or one year into lessons. If you set reading aside initially and introduce it in small increments you can use the extra lesson time to teach rhythm, metre, dynamics, singing and other fantastic skills that will serve your students much better in the long run.

Any time you do feel frustrated or impatient with your student's progress, ask yourself:

- Are they making some progress, at least in certain areas?
- Is the student happy?
- Are the parents happy?

If the answers here are yes, yes and yes then you just need to have a chat with *yourself*, adjust your own expectations and focus on enjoying making music with your students.

Carina put this very simply and beautifully in our interview: "I don't care about how small the steps are that we're taking. I'm happy when there is progress. I'm unhappy when there's not."

FORGETTING THAT YOU'RE AN ADULT

All the best preschool teachers I know step into their student's world in each and every lesson. You may have a mortgage and sensible clothes and many "grown up" responsibilities, but when you teach little ones you need to leave those at the door and keep in mind the two core principles of the preschooler's universe: curiosity and play.

Sometimes it's our adulty instinct to fight against these tendencies. When they're curious about something that's not on the agenda, we have the urge to force them back to the topic at hand. And when they want to play or experiment with something in a different way than we expected, we try to course-correct.

Now, let me be clear: I'm not saying you should follow the kiddo wherever they choose to go. If they're drawn to something that is truly irrelevant we need to steer them back to music. What I am saying, though, is that we need to follow our students' natural curiosities. We shouldn't just let them pick up random ornaments and discuss the physics of snow globes with us, but we should let them try out each of the piano pedals and listen to the effect it has, even if it wasn't on the agenda that day.

Don't let your inhibitions hold you back. Laugh, be silly, crawl around on the floor and enjoy floating into the preschool universe during your preschool lessons. It's a fun place to hang out if you can let go of the gravitational pull of adulthood.

Kris emphasises the importance of playfulness to a successful preschool piano lesson: "My number one tip is that it's OK to be silly and you should be able to. You have to be a bit of an entertainer. Make faces or make funny sounds. Use puppets. Use whatever it takes to engage the child in the lesson."

Children love learning when they're allowed to explore. It's our job to facilitate their natural affinity for play. Playfulness is so important, in fact, that it gets a whole chapter all to itself.

PART 2
During the lessons

When I first started teaching as a teenager, I felt I had to appear more serious in order for parents to think I was responsible. I put on my babysitting voice, my most respectable clothes and, unfortunately, quite a serious personality too.

Don't get me wrong: I wasn't harsh or unpleasant to the kids in any way. They all liked me and we had good relationships...but I wasn't exactly fun. The trouble was that I was hesitant to get involved in the process with them. I was too self-conscious and thought too much about what the parents could hear from the other room.

Everything changed as soon as I started teaching pre-schoolers. I lost my inhibitions and got on the ground with my students to play, sang along even though my voice wasn't spectacular, and trotted around the room like a horse when necessary. It was my preschool students who taught me to get out of my own way and become absorbed in the learning process. When I started teaching preschoolers there was no longer any choice; I had to get a bit silly and learn how to play or they would not be able to learn. Simple as that.

This playfulness has carried over into all my lessons, and every one of my students has benefited. So, if you dive into this section and start to find that some of the suggested activities are pushing you out of your mental comfort zone, please consider throwing caution to the wind and just giving them a go. You're sure to learn something along the way even if they don't become a regular part of your lessons.

Chapter 3
PLAYING

"Play is the work of the child."
Maria Montessori

If you can, spend some time observing a preschool-aged child (hopefully you know one) in their natural environment. What do they do when they're hanging out?

- They pick things up and examine them closely from all sides.
- They put different objects together, often in ways that don't work, and sometimes in surprising ways that do work.
- They "test" things by tapping them or trying to pull them apart.
- They have conversations with inanimate objects or imaginary creatures, often imitating adult conversations that they have heard.

If you only glance, you'll simply see a child playing, and it's easy to write this off as just "messing about". But this is serious work. Children didn't evolve with this propensity for play just for larks. It's a very important part of their development.

I think the quote from Maria Montessori above says it all, so I'll say it again: "Play is the work of the child." Play is how children socialise, understand the world, problem-solve and learn to use their bodies. If we try to set play aside and create a lesson environment we are missing the whole point. Play is the educational environment for a preschooler. We can, and should, find playfulness in everything we do so that we can harness the learning superpowers of young children.

PLAYING USING STORIES AND IMAGINATION

We adults can't access the superpower of play as easily and instinctively as children can. For many of us, it's buried in the back corner of our brains, and it may need some dusting off. One way you can learn to use this superpower (no matter how thick the layer of dust on your 'playing' file) is to tell a story. This strategy can be used to introduce or practise any conceivable concept. Let me give you a couple of examples.

One of the common confusions that young students struggle with is the idea of high sounds and low sounds. There are two issues with this. Firstly, we're describing sounds using words that they know to mean something else: high means *up* high and low means *down* low. The second leap is to then place these on the piano, with high sounds on the right and low sounds on the left.

An easy way to teach this, and re-teach it as many times as necessary, is to use animal stories. Play some high sounds on the piano and ask your student what animal makes these kinds of high sounds. Maybe they'll say it sounds like a mouse squeaking. Then play low sounds and ask your student what animal makes low sounds like this. Perhaps they'll say it sounds like an elephant. You can then make up a story about these animals and ask your student to play the corresponding high or low sounds when the animals speak.

"An elephant was walking through the rainforest with his friends and trumpeting happily to them (point and gesture for your student to play low sounds) *as he went. Suddenly, he heard a tiny sound* (point and gesture for your student to play high sounds) *and felt teeny tiny footsteps on his head. The elephant groaned in confusion* (point and gesture for your student to play low sounds) *and tried to figure out what this squeaking was.*

As he twisted and turned trying to see his own head the squeaks got louder (point and gesture for your student to play high sounds) *and louder* (point and gesture for your student to play high sounds) *and louder* (point and gesture for your student to play high sounds) *until they were right inside his ear! He trumpeted loudly* (point and gesture for your student to play low sounds) *with his trunk and shook his head to try and get rid of his unwanted guest. Back and forth it went: trumpet* (point and gesture for your student to play low sounds), *squeak* (point and gesture for your student to play high sounds), *trumpet* (point and gesture for your student to play low sounds), *squeak* (point and gesture for your student to play high sounds), *until suddenly there was one big squeak* (point and gesture for your student to play high sounds) *and the elephant saw a mouse fall at his feet and run away into the forest."*

These stories can change week to week as your student comes up with different animals and can be used to teach any pair of opposites, such as loud vs soft, same vs different, short vs long, etc.

Notice a few important details in the above example:

- The student is involved in the creation of the story. By using the animal suggestions they provide, you are basing the exercise on their existing understanding of the concepts and expanding from there, rather than working off a pre-rehearsed script.
- The student is not asked whether a sound is 'high' or 'low'. This type of vocabulary can be picked up naturally from our using the words in context.
- We're not quizzing the student about where the high and low sounds are on the piano; we're pointing to the correct side of the piano each time so that our student can be successful and learn by doing.

Everything in the exercise is structured so that the student gets to interact with the idea and experiment so that they can forge their own pathways to understanding. Knowledge gained in this way will be more flexible, and your student will be able to apply it in different contexts, not just in the exact way they learned it.

Now let's take a completely different example, this time in the area of technique. One of the things we want for all our students (no matter which school of technique, if any, we follow) is for them to play without tension. Sometimes, tension can creep into the body in strange ways. Often, when we ask young students to raise their wrist, for example, their shoulders will rise up too. Preschool-aged children can't always distinguish between different body parts.

We can see evidence of this when a child feels sick or hurt. At age three or four they won't always be able to tell you *where* it hurts. They may point to the wrong leg, not because the scrape on the other knee doesn't hurt, but because they can't quite organise, place or describe these feelings yet.

So let's say we have a student who has a habit of scrunching her shoulders all the way up to her ears, and it's causing tension throughout her arm which is affecting her playing. We need a story that's going to engage her playing superpowers and make the feeling of relaxed shoulders easier to recall and execute.

Ask your student whether she's ever seen a stringed puppet. What happens when we pull the strings up? What happens when we let them go? Tell her that she is a puppet and she has a string attached to each of her shoulders. Mime tying a string to each of her shoulders while you explain this. Then stand facing each other and tell her that you're holding the strings. Pull the imaginary strings up slowly, higher and higher, until her shoulders are raised up as high as they can go. Then suddenly let go of the strings. If she doesn't immediately drop her shoulders down, ask her again about what happens when we let go of the puppet strings. Do puppets hold up their shoulders on their own? Repeat this a few times and then ask her to sit at the piano and imagine the puppet strings being pulled up and dropped down before she plays. Draw a picture of a puppet that she can use to remind her of this routine at home.

In this exercise, we didn't allow our student to choose as many of the parameters as we did in the elephant and mouse story since we needed quite a specific example. But we did allow her to discover parts of the story for herself and interact with it. We didn't say: "When the strings are dropped the puppet's shoulders fall down, so that's what you must do with yours." Instead, we asked questions and allowed her to experience the movements before she had all the answers.

Using stories and our students' imaginations, we can make experiences much more likely to stick in their memories. Taking this approach might sometimes feel like more effort and overly time consuming, but, if you engage with students in this way rather than telling them facts or giving them explanations, you will repeat yourself less and save time and energy in the long run.

Plus, if you get into it (remember, you'll need to shed some of your adult-ness to do so), it's far more fun for you too.

PLAYING WITH MANIPULATIVES AND TOYS

If play is the work of the child, toys are their tools. We can do a whole lot without them, using only the superpower of imagination, but toys can be a great aid in the development of a preschooler's skills. By teaching through manipulatives you can help your student learn coordination and dexterity at the same time as getting them to interact with concepts we need them to understand.

The simplest things can be used as toys in your preschool lessons. Clothes pegs, for example, are a great way to improve finger control. You can use them for any matching game by having your student put the peg on the correct answer. They could be selecting between letters, numbers, animals, symbols, patterns, or any number of things you need to practise together.

Balls are another cheap and simple toy that can be used for a variety of purposes. Passing the ball on the beat is a good way to work on steady pulse with young students and you can do this while singing together or listening to music. (Bouncing a ball on the beat is another good way to practise this but it's a more sophisticated movement and is usually best saved for slightly older children.) Stress balls made of foam or soft rubber are a good way to develop finger strength and can be great for keeping a wiggly child's hands occupied while they listen.

Putty and playdough can be used to create shapes and

"draw" things that you're working on. You can create simple patterns, such as circle–ring–circle–ring, and ask your student to make the shape that goes next. This helps them to build their understanding of repeating patterns, which is very important in music, and they get the tactile experience of creating with putty which improves their coordination.

Bringing puppets and stuffed animals into your stories will make them come alive for your preschool student. You can also use characters like these to help your student understand patterns in music by assigning one to each element in the pattern. Tell a preschooler that the piece is in ABA form and you will probably get a wide blank stare in return. Explain that 'Eric the Antelope' sings first, then 'Kara the Koala' answers, and then 'Eric the Antelope' sings again, and they'll pick it up pretty quickly.

Lyndel uses butterfly finger puppets in her studio to work on technique. (*Vibrant Music Teaching* members can watch the video with her demonstration in the Video Library.) The puppets have floaty organza wings and this gives her a wonderful, playful and evocative way to talk about technique. Once her students see the butterfly floating around they know the kind of technique she's looking for, and when they get stiff all it takes is a quick reminder of "Where are your butterflies?" to get them moving more freely again.

I've saved my favourite toy–tool for last: crayons. When I start working with a new preschool student and they take a crayon from me with confidence – like they've done it a thousand times before – I know they'll make speedy progress in their piano lessons. These kids, who have obviously done plenty of colouring at home, have more refined control of their fingers, a longer attention span and a better understanding of patterns. This isn't based on any scientific study, and I can't say how much is correlation (children who have a natural talent for these skills enjoy colouring) and how much causation (children develop these skills through colouring), but, nevertheless, I think bringing colouring into your lessons can only be a good thing. Take any opportunity in the lesson to get your student to circle, make lines and draw pictures themselves. It will take longer than you doing it but you will get more learning baked into the exercise, and whatever you're trying to work on with them will be retained for longer.

PLAYING TO FACILITATE DISCOVERY

Whether you use stories or toys or other playful aspects, it's all about you and your student exploring together. Play is not just a way to placate a child and keep them having fun; it's a tool that you can use with intention and a clear purpose.

We need to allow our students to discover answers themselves. Don't tell your student that it won't sound good if they play certain notes together; allow them to improvise and discuss what they find. Don't give them tricks for remembering the music alphabet in reverse; play with them and come up with a silly song together that they can practise.

Allow them to take ownership of their learning with you as the guide.

Chapter 4
SITTING

"Never bend your head. Always hold it high. Look the world straight in the eye."
Helen Keller

Cast your mind back to that image of you sitting at the toofpranie again and really take a moment to feel the whole setup.

You walk into the studio and are asked to sit up in front of the toofpranie. The bench is about 120cm (4ft) off the ground and the toofpranie is about 245cm (8ft) wide. The bench is almost shoulder height but you clamber up as best you can and stare down the enormous keys.

Every time your teacher asks you to play middle Γ you're not only grasping to figure out where on earth this key is but also physically grasping to stay perched on the bench because your legs are dangling way above the ground and you keep nearly slipping off. You can barely see from one side of the toofpranie to the other, let alone see it clearly enough to navigate and play successfully.

How do you feel? Comfortable? At ease? If you really visualise this fully, you will see that it's a pretty intimidating scenario. We need to do everything we can to make our littlest students feel stable and relaxed when they're sitting at this instrument that was essentially designed for an adult man.

SITTING AT THE RIGHT BENCH HEIGHT

The first thing to make sure of is that the bench is at the correct height for your young student. As mentioned in the notes about equipment above, you'll need a bench that goes up to a height of about 60cm (24in).

Every child is different and, since the height of the bench really depends more on torso length than standing height, it will take some getting used to before you're able to set it up right on the first go. Don't feel that this setting up time is "wasted". It's essential that you set your preschool student up correctly so that they can learn to play with good technique from a stable position. Spend a few minutes at the start of the lesson getting this right and tweaking the bench height until it's correct. Involve your student by having them place their hands on the keys (without playing) and talk about how we need to find the height that gives them a straight line with their forearms, parallel to the floor. If the parent is there, involve them in this process too and encourage them to take a photo when the setup is correct so that they can get everything in a good position at home.

SITTING WITHOUT DANGLING FEET

Picture sitting at the toofpranie one more time. You're 120cm (4ft) off the ground – that's higher than a kitchen counter. Wouldn't you want somewhere to put your feet?

The footstool you use for your preschool students doesn't have to be fancy, but it does have to be sturdy and sufficiently tall. Whatever you choose, whether that's a plastic box or a top-of-the-range pedal extender, it needs to provide a comfortable base for your students and be able to withstand a little wriggling and shuffling without toppling over.

Oh, and if the imaginary feeling of your own uncomfortable dangling feet at the toofpranie isn't enough to persuade you that you need a footstool, do it to protect your piano. Dangling feet + wiggly preschooler = kicked piano.

SITTING...BUT NOT FOR TOO LONG!

Even the most comfortable bench and stool setup will start to get uncomfortable for a preschooler after about 3–5 minutes. Remember how I said that attention span is not an issue? Well, it will be if you keep them plonked on the bench. Any time your student starts getting off topic or ignoring your directions, or their eyes start to wander towards those sparkling objects, your first thought should be: we need to MOVE!

Chapter 5
MOVING

"The more technique you have, the less you have to worry about it. The more technique there is, the less there is."
Pablo Picasso

If we're not going to stay sitting for most of the lesson, we'll need to find ways to move around and wiggle about. As well as getting off the bench to play games, your preschooler will need to do lots of gross motor activities to practise moving in time and fine motor activities to develop dexterity.

MOVING TO THE BEAT

Have you ever had an older student who didn't seem to have any sense of a steady beat? They couldn't clap, march, or play with the pulse? This can take a lot of work to fix with a 10-year-old and can stall their progress in other areas, and it basically comes down (like most things) to a lack of practice. Many kids will be exposed to enough music and have enough instinctive feeling for it that they will be able to tap along, but some won't without conscious and guided practice.

Fortunately for us, it's much easier to develop this skill in 3–5-year-olds. It may take them a while to get it, but when they start music lessons this young we have the luxury of time. They have 5–7 years before they become that 10-year-old who wants to learn the latest pop song or Für Elise to impress their friends. And, by the time they get there (and long before that), they will have a rock-steady sense of pulse and understanding of rhythm – if we do our jobs right and invest the time now.

Until your student can reliably tap or march along to the beat independently, every single lesson should include some kind of movement to a beat. Put together a playlist of music in a variety of metres with a strong pulse and a slow-to-medium tempo. Move to the music at each lesson in a variety of ways:

- Marching
- Patsching (tapping your lap with both hands)
- Clapping[2]
- Sidestepping
- Swaying
- Touching your toes
- Tapping your shoulders
- Dancing with scarves
- Drumming
- Stayin' Alive (you know the dance move I mean...if you don't, look it up!)

It's important to mix things up and move in different ways, not only to keep things fresh, but also to

---

2 Clapping is more difficult for young children than patsching, marching and other movements listed here, so use it more sparingly, especially when students are having trouble staying in time.

develop in your students a more thorough under-standing and feeling for the pulse that they can apply in different scenarios. You can also incorporate this pulse work into singing games which we'll talk about in the 'Singing' chapter.

MOVING IN BIG WAYS

We will have more success with smaller movements if we start with big ones first. The actions for practis-ing moving to the pulse will be helpful for develop-ing these gross motor skills but it's also beneficial to create a technical warmup routine that starts with big stretches and movements.

Playing the piano is a physical activity, and I believe starting with some sort of movement activ-ity or stretches to loosen up and become aware of our bodies is a good habit for us all to get into. But it's especially important for young children. When you're barely aware that you have wrists, or that you can move your shoulders without creating tension in your arms, it's hard to work on the specific move-ments and techniques needed to play piano well. We will explore this more when we talk about mirroring in the 'Copying' chapter, but for now I will just say that it's a good idea to develop a structured move-ment sequence with your student that they can also do at home before they practise. Try this routine for starters and incorporate other movements based on your own goals:

- Swing your arms around, letting them flop

against your sides.

- Lift your arms up and let them fall down loosely by your sides. Repeat this three times.
- Scrunch your shoulders up to your ears and then roll them back and down. Repeat this three times.
- Hold one palm up facing outwards (as if about to give someone a high five) and gently stretch the fingers back with your other hand. Repeat on the other side.
- Do wrist circles.
- Make circles with your nose.
- Do a forward fold (reaching towards your toes) and sway from side to side.

Each of these moves has its own specific benefits but they all share one common goal: to bring awareness to different parts of the body and how we use them. When we do this exercise consistently with our students before they sit up at the piano it can make a big difference to how they move for the rest of the lesson or practice session.

MOVING IN LITTLE WAYS

Most 3–5-year-olds will not yet have developed fine control over their fingers when they start lessons with you. They will probably only be able to reliably lift their finger 2 on its own, and, when asked to use the other fingers individually, many will use their other hand to pull up individual fingers or help control them. This fact, combined with the size of their hands, makes a five-finger position with one finger on each key out of the question in the beginning stages. Even if they do manage to contort their hand to span five keys, they will almost always be introducing a lot of tension into their hand and arm in order to do so.

Rather than rush to play with all their fingers in this way I prefer to let preschool students use one finger only from each hand (most will default to finger 2 but finger 3 works well also) for at least the first semester, if not the first year or more, of their lessons. During this time, we can work to develop dexterity away from the piano through finger rhymes and games. Here are a couple of my favourite fingerplays that you and your student can do together:

Ten Flamingos
Ten flamingos standing tall,
(hold up hands)
Till one tires and has to fall.
(drop one finger down)
Nine flamingos standing tall,
Till one tires and has to fall.
(continue until you only have one finger left)
One flamingo standing tall,
Till it tires and there's no more.
(close hand and then show open palms)

Dancing Fingers
Dancing fingers in the air,
(wiggle fingers in the air)
Dancing fingers in my hair,
(wiggle fingers on top of head)

Dancing fingers on my knees,
(wiggle fingers on knees)
Dancing fingers on the keys.
(wiggle fingers on the piano, playing lightly)

You can find more of these games in printable format, along with videos of the actions plus lots more bonuses that go with this book, at: vibrantmusicteaching. com/play

Other games that involve tapping fingertips on a table, wiggling fingers or using finger puppets are great to combine with these types of fingerplays, and they're the perfect thing for parents (even parents without any musical training) to do with their child at home. The main thing to remember is that you're not in a rush for them to play scales or develop some particular technique. Keep things playful and everything else will follow in time.

Chapter 6
SEEING

"The question is not what you look at, but what you see."
Henry David Thoreau

For preschool students, a lot of the confusions that can arise are down to the fact that they're simply not seeing what we're seeing.

Our adult brains are so keenly refined for seeing patterns that we can look at a piano and automatically categorise the black keys into two groups: the twos and the threes. Even with an older student, who might not be able to immediately make this mental map of the piano, if we say "C is to the left of the two black keys", they will be able to apply and assimilate this new way of seeing the patterns on the piano.

Not so for a preschooler. Not only are they not defaulting to this mode of categorisation, but they're not even seeing the patterns yet. And if they can't see those patterns, finding C on the piano is just like finding middle Γ on the toofpranie: basically impossible.

SEEING PATTERNS

In order to help them see these types of patterns, we need to give our preschool students something to latch on to. They need associations with concepts they already understand and feel confident with so that they can build upon that base.

Manipulatives and toys can be very useful for this. By giving our students little tokens that they can place on top of the different groups of black keys, or move along a pattern that is ascending, or place on top of any other pattern we need them to see, we are giving them a foothold. It's no longer two things they have never heard of or seen before (i.e. a seemingly random group of piano keys plus the phrase "three black key group"); it's simply a case of giving new meaning to an old friend. This is what I do with my dog and frog cards which sit on top of the black key groups. I'm giving a new meaning to dogs and frogs within the context of piano lessons. And the association makes sense as they can physically move the dogs and frogs around and see which keys they fit. (*Vibrant Music Teaching* members can find these in the library; non-members can download them at: vibrantmusicteaching.com/play)

Whenever your preschooler is having trouble with a new concept, do a quick check-in with this idea. Is there a pattern involved that your adult brain is automatically seeing that maybe your preschooler is missing? If so, can you think of a way to come up with associations to help them interact with the pattern and see it in a new way?

SEEING SYMBOLS

Whether it's numbers, letters, notes or dynamics, there are certain symbols and characters that we will need our students to recognise if we're going to bridge the gap towards reading or pre-reading material. We'll talk more about the pros and cons of reading, and of the different systems, in the 'Reading' chapter, but for now let's assume that you want your student to learn some of the written elements they'll need to read music successfully. When's the best time to introduce these signs and how should we do it?

You may have heard of the "sound before symbol" approach to teaching music. I think this is a good general mantra to follow for our preschool lessons, although I would adjust it slightly: "sound *and movement* before symbol". I think it's so important that preschool students get to use their bodies to internalise a concept – whether that's through marching, playing or singing – before they ever go near its symbol.

When you do introduce a new sign or symbol, whatever it is, try to get students to do three things:

1. **Match it to something they already know.** For example, match a card with a 4-beat note on it to a set of four animals.

2. **Describe it.** I do this by asking my students to guide me while I draw the symbol. What should I do first? Should I colour in the circle or leave it unfilled? Where does the next line go?

3. **Draw it.** You can either guide them or allow them to use a picture as a reference, but I would suggest they draw free-hand rather than trace. The more they have to think for themselves, the better they'll retain the knowledge.

Don't worry if their drawings are not very accurate! Kris knows that her students are learning even when they draw something that's not exactly what she prescribed: "If they draw a staff and it has 20 lines, I like to joke that it looks like early Gregorian chant. I would say: 'Well, perhaps that child is going to be the inventor of what will become standard notation!' You just never know, right?"

Repeating these activities over time will give your students a more flexible ability to recognise and name the symbol later.

Most of all, though, don't fuss too much over names and signs. We can provide a much richer music education than just labels and shapes.

Chapter 7
COPYING

*"Imitation is not just the sincerest form of flattery —
it's the sincerest form of learning."*
George Bernard Shaw

Have you ever seen a young animal learning from its mother? They watch first and then they try it – clumsily at first. But then they watch again and try again. This is how humans learn too. We need to see examples that we can imitate. The skills we learn, though, are sometimes so complex that they need to be broken down into their component parts. It's good for students to see the "finished product", such as a complete piece or a beautiful legato technique, but, unlike an orangutan teaching her kiddo to swing through the trees, we need to allow for imitation in minute incremental stages.

COPYING PATTERNS

Most piano lessons with preschoolers will involve less reading than those with older students (we'll talk about this more in the 'Reading' chapter) and so some or all music will be taught by rote. If the idea of rote teaching leaves a bad taste in your mouth, you're not alone. Some associate the idea of teaching by rote with monotonous chanting of historical dates in classrooms or other such disconnected and disengaging styles of teaching. Others will have encountered students who seem to have learned entirely by rote and not only cannot read music but seem to have no real awareness of what they're doing when they're playing.

However, all rote teaching means is learning by imitation rather than from written music. Students learn by watching the teacher play short sections of the piece and then trying it themselves. Through this process they absorb not only the piece itself but also the quality of their teacher's movement and how they bring the music to life.

Rote pieces should be highly patterned so that they are easy to imitate and remember. These pieces are often easier than they look and sound; when we don't have to be concerned with how difficult the notation would be to read, we can explore much more of the piano. They can be extremely satisfying for beginners of all ages as they can get a full rich sound right from the start.

Teaching by rote has a valuable place in our studios when we do it with intention, and it's an especially useful strategy for teaching preschoolers.

COPYING THE WAY YOU MOVE

Most preschoolers barely even know where their wrists are and yet, to play piano well, they will need to have finely tuned control over their arms, wrists, hands and fingers. Following our lead is the best way for them to develop these skills. As well as regularly demonstrating the technique we want for our students, and directing their attention when we do, it's useful to warm up at the start of your lessons with a mirroring exercise. Stand facing your student and ask them to follow your lead:

- Raise your shoulders up and drop them down.
- Lift your arms up and let them fall by your sides.
- Do wrist circles.
- Hold your fingers up one at a time.

These simple activities, and others that are relevant to what you need your student to focus on that day, can bring your student's awareness to their body and how they use it, and can make a big difference to how the rest of the lesson goes.

COPYING TROUBLESHOOTING

One difficulty you may come across with some preschool students is their apparent disinterest in copying your actions. Although student-led play and discovery are important, we also need students to imitate us from time to time in order to learn. If you have a student who is refusing to play back a phrase you played or clap what you just clapped, this normally comes down to one of two things:

1. It's too hard and, instead of setting themselves up for failure, they're opting not to try.
2. They don't trust you or have a strong enough relationship with you yet.

The first reason is the most common and the solution is simple: make it easier. Keep making it easier until they are able to imitate what you did. For example, if you were playing a short section of a rote piece and they were not playing it back, try playing just one note and asking them to play it back. If they still don't play, or they play an incorrect note, try pointing to the correct key on the piano or playing it as a "team", with you holding their hand or with their hand sitting on top of yours. If it still doesn't work, then you probably have the second issue…

Working on our relationships with our older students is instinctive. We know without conscious thought that we need to develop a rapport with another adult in order for them to trust our judgement, feel comfortable in their lessons and make good progress. But we can too easily neglect our relationships with our younger students. If they don't like you, they won't want to be like you, and they won't copy what you did. Harsh but true.

Once you recognise this problem, it's pretty easy to fix. Ask about your student's interests and follow up with them at the next lesson. Take care to pick out stickers and toys, and tailor your stories, based on what they love. Do dinosaur themed lessons or find a sloth toy to keep them company at the piano. In other words, make friends with your preschool student and get to know them. Being little does not mean they have a small personality!

And, above all else, be genuine. Don't think that

because they haven't mastered buttoning clothes up or tying their shoelaces yet that they're not people-savvy. Your preschool student will see right through platitudes and straight-up lies, and it will have a negative effect on your relationship.

Fast forward to the end of your toofpranie lesson in Grownupville and imagine the whole thing went as poorly as those first few minutes (we'll come back to the details later). You get to the end of that grueling and confusing lesson, you're finally heading out the door, and you experience this exchange:

> "How did you get on?" asks your boss. But before you can answer the teacher jumps in with: "Oh, wonderful! Great first lesson."
>
> Great first lesson? Is she kidding?! She's either a liar or not as smart as she looks because that was terrible. You go home feeling bewildered and incompetent. You're never going to be able to play the toofpranie, you think. It's just too hard.

Isn't this how you would feel? We can't talk to preschoolers exactly the same way we talk to adults, but the sentiment behind what we say can be the same. We can and should be honest, empathetic and understanding at all times. That's the best way to develop relationships with any human being, whether they're 4 or 48.

Chapter 8
READING

"Never trust anyone who has not brought a book with them."
Lemony Snicket

Reading can be a contentious issue, and I don't want to hand down a judgement from on high about whether or not to include it in lessons with young beginners. But I will let you know where I stand. I believe very strongly that reading should not be the *centre* of preschool piano lessons. I believe, less vociferously, that it's beneficial to include some reading or reading preparation work in your preschool piano teaching.

READING...OR NOT?

Let's go through the pros and cons more thoroughly.

On one side of the debate, there are those who have seen students who learnt entirely by ear or rote and reach quite an advanced level without being able to read well. This is certainly a concern, as I believe that what all of us want is to create holistic musicians. Our students should be able to improvise, perform, read and write music – just as their school teachers want them to be able to converse, recite, read and write in their native language. The fear is that if we spend too long working without notation their ears will get "too good" and their reading will always be lagging behind. On the other side of the debate, however, there is a strong argument for delaying reading based on the parallel with how we learn our native language. We don't start by teaching a newborn baby the alphabet, and then have them learn to slowly sound out individual words, before we eventually let them come up with their own sentences. They learn to speak first, and they learn by listening. When they eventually learn to read, they learn sight-words and how to write letters in conjunction with reading. Shouldn't our students first listen, imitate and create their own music before learning to read and write notation?

So, the question is, are we holding back students' music reading in the long term by delaying its introduction? And, if we can agree that it's possible to delay reading for some length of time without this having a detrimental effect, how long is too long?

Our toofpranie lesson in Grownupville is focused entirely on reading. Let's pick up where we left off in the 'Forgetting' chapter.

You've just played through that extremely dull piece made up entirely of middle Γ.

Now the teacher turns the page to reveal the next piece.

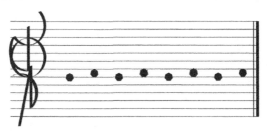

"Right", she says, "this next note is burdle Δ (delta) and it's just after middle Γ on the toofpranie."

OK, you think, you can just about follow that. But then she goes on...

"And the teans with the dotted line on the outside are called upsuls. Upsuls last for two keps."

She asks you to play the piece and stands pointing to the first note and looking at you expectantly again, so you jump to attention and look at the toofpranie to try and find middle Γ. You can't be sure, but you think it was round about...here?

Nope. Wrong again. She moves your hand to a different key on the toofpranie and says firmly: "Middle Γ is **here**." Her face is puzzled, verging on annoyed now. You do your best to play through the song but you keep forgetting about the upsuls so she repeats her instruction that they last for two keps and you try the song several more times until she seems satisfied and turns the page again.

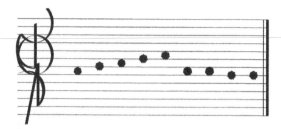

"After burdle Δ are burdle E (epsilon), Z (zeta) and H (eta)," she says, pointing to them on the page. "The upsuls with the rounded dotted lines are actually martoes. Martoes last for five keps."

This guessing game is really getting stressful now. You look down at the toofpranie and make another stab at finding middle Γ.

"No," she says, pointing more forcefully to the first tean. "This piece starts on burdle Δ, not middle Γ. See?"

So you did finally find middle Γ correctly then. Do you not at least get credit for that?! You're starting to think this woman is pretty unreasonable but you struggle through the rest of the piece as best you can.

It's almost the end of your 145-minute lesson but the teacher has one more task in store. She takes out a pack of flashcards and shows you one at a time.

"What's this?" she asks.

"Urm...a tean?" you answer hesitantly.

"Good," she says. "And this?"

"An upsul."

"No," she says, furrowing her brow. "It's a martoe. What about this?"

"Middle Γ?"

"No," she sighs, "that's burdle E. How about this one, then?"

Just as you're about to take another random guess the doorbell rings. Thank goodness! This impossible pop quiz is finally over.

There are many different ways to approach reading and thankfully it doesn't have to be as dry as this toofpranie lesson. But, no matter what method you use to teach reading, you will run the risk of it taking over the whole lesson with a preschool student because you can't make the same leaps in understanding that you can with older students. It needs to be handled with care and with your priorities for your preschool students firmly in mind.

So where will you land on the reading question? We each need to find our own balance between reading and other approaches to making music with our preschoolers. The one thing I will caution against is reading on the staff right away and making this the core of what you do in your lessons, with the other activities branching off from there. This may be how you're used to piano lessons looking...but all the more reason to question it. Never do something because you should or because that's just how it's done.

I said at the beginning of this chapter that I did believe in introducing some reading preparation work in preschool lessons. For me, there is so much to be done in lessons that this is just one small component. I do think it's valuable, however, to introduce some patterning work, to start to build the association between up/down the page and high/low on the piano, and to develop the concept that one symbol represents one sound. Each method book geared towards preschoolers will take a different approach and, while I don't want to mention any specific method books here, I will go through the broad categories so that you will be able to look at the books for yourself and quickly understand what they're doing and why they're doing it.

READING WITH LETTER NAMES

Some beginner music books use letter names either inside the note heads or underneath the notes to help students find their way around. This is my least favourite pre-reading aid for preschool students for a couple of reasons:

- Preschoolers don't know or aren't that confident with the alphabet yet, making this another thing to learn rather than a helping hand.
- This approach encourages students to think in terms of individual notes rather than patterns.

It's that second point that causes me to immediately put a method book back down if I see letter names used as a reading aid. Even if a preschooler does know their letters backwards, forwards and upside-down, I don't want them to think of each note on its own, floating in space, disconnected from the others. It's true that sometimes we will need to figure out a note name and where it is on the piano. This note-by-note approach is similar to sounding out words letter by letter when reading language, and it's a useful fall-back option. But most of the time when we see a word we immediately recognise it as one complete concept. This is why children learn sight-words in school and why they should learn to see patterns in music too. It's much more efficient and leads to a better understanding of music than thinking in individual notes can allow.

READING WITH FINGER NUMBERS

Probably the most common pre-reading approach taken in method books (not just ones for preschoolers) is finger numbers. These are normally laid out as notes that ascend and descend as if on a staff (but with no staff lines) with the finger numbers either above or below to show right or left hand.

This system has several advantages. It shows the directionality of notes without including any extra information that the student doesn't really need in the beginning, such as staff lines, clefs, barlines, etc. It also helps students to learn:

- Finger numbers
- One note = one symbol
- Note values

And, in many books, this system is used to teach songs on the black keys, which are easier to navigate for beginner students but might be tricky to teach from standard notation in the key of G flat.

This all sounds good, but reading by finger numbers has its limitations. Students can come to think in positions if they play this way for too long. In their minds, the steps to playing a song are: find the right spot, place fingers there, and play without moving from that spot. This can lead to students getting "stuck" to the keys and developing a playing technique or mindset that is too rigid.

Not all students will think that way, however, and this tendency can be avoided if teachers are careful and make good use of rote pieces that explore the whole keyboard. The biggest limitation of the finger number reading method for preschoolers is that students need to be in a five-finger position to play many of these pieces. As discussed in the 'Moving' chapter, I prefer to let young students use one finger in the beginning so that they don't stretch their hand and introduce tension in order to control their weaker fingers. For this reason, while I do occasionally use finger number reading pieces, I only do so with slightly older students or with those who have been with me for a little while and have already developed good technique. I don't see this as a good first step for 3–5-year-olds.

READING WITH CHARACTERS

A few method books take the fun and playful approach of using cartoon characters to aid the development of reading skills. This is normally used in conjunction with one of the approaches above: the characters can either represent letters (Amy the Ant for A and Clarissa the Cat for C, for example) or fingers. So this system really ends up with the same pros and cons as the systems discussed above but with one added pro: it's usually easier for preschoolers to remember Clarissa the Cat than the letter C. Most of them will have met a cat before, and few will have any fondness or associations with the shape of the letter C, and so the character approach does have a distinct advantage in terms of how easily the students will be able to retain the knowledge.

READING WITH COLOURS

The simplest method of making reading more accessible for preschoolers is to add colour. Young children can quickly and easily grasp the relationship between seeing the red shape and playing the red key. At its most basic level there is no new symbol they need to learn to read in this way. They will need to learn where the red key is, of course, but it's easy to scaffold this learning by using removable sticky tabs or placing a red token on the key and gradually removing this aid when your student is ready.

If you're going to stay away from traditional reading for a considerable amount of time, this is my preferred reading method – not just because of its accessibility for preschoolers but also because they can use any finger they wish to play these pieces. This provides lots more opportunities to practise using the whole arm to play, since they need to hop from key to key, and I see it as a great complement to learning pieces by rote and by ear. If the coloured notation is shown on a staff or a simplified staff, they're also absorbing the idea that music is read from left to right and that the notes go up and down based on pitch.

Ultimately, reading should be a small part of your preschool lessons. If you are going to include it, pick the system that makes the most sense to you. Maybe that's colours; maybe it's characters. Whatever it is, don't do too much of it.

Chapter 9
SINGING

"The only thing better than singing is more singing."
Ella Fitzgerald

We have an instrument baked into our bodies and it makes sense that, if we're going to learn an external instrument, we should also understand this internal one. Experiencing music theory ideas and concepts through singing is one of the most natural, instinctive and enjoyable ways to learn. Most children will sing and dance along to music without being told to and without thinking about it. If we embrace the voice in our preschool lessons we can use it to explore a whole host of topics and to practise skills that our students can use at the piano.

SINGING IN TUNE

The first hurdle to overcome when you want to use singing as a teaching tool is that some students cannot sing...yet. I truly believe almost anyone can sing if given enough practice, but some students at this age do struggle to match pitch and will need some extra help to find their singing voice.

To help students with pitch, and singing in general, you can do some fun explorations together in each lesson. Try making the sounds of different siren and animal noises and drawing squiggles and lines like these on a whiteboard or a page to follow with your voices.

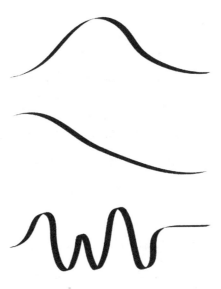

It can also be helpful to follow these vocal shapes with your body. For example, show the sound you're making by drawing the line in the air together, or crouch down on the floor when singing low sounds and stretch up to the sky when singing high sounds.

If, after lots of these types of exercises, you have a child who is still not singing on pitch, please don't worry about it. They will probably find their singing voice in time; they're simply not at that stage yet. But, as Kris points out, this doesn't mean that you shouldn't keep singing together: "They're not necessarily going to sing on pitch. I think that's an unrealistic expectation. Some of them will. Some of them won't. But are they singing along and having a good time? Are they singing in the rhythm of the song? If that's the case, they're taking away the knowledge of the rhythm and feeling it."

SINGING AND MOVING

Singing and moving at the same time can help students internalise concepts like pulse, rhythm and pitch. Many folk songs have fun actions that focus on a specific skill while feeling like a game to the student. For example, the simple action song below gives kids great practice at moving to the beat, and they can even make up their own actions to create additional verses.

In Seesaw, we hold hands with a partner and lift and lower their arms to act out the up-and-down motion of a seesaw while following the pitch of the song.

There are hundreds of games like this. For more ideas, I recommend looking up *Kodály Hub*, where songs and game descriptions are available to teachers for free.

SINGING WITH SOLFA

If you're just getting started with singing in your piano lessons, incorporating solfa may feel like a bigger jump than you're willing to take right now. When you're ready, though, bringing solfa into your lessons can be a fantastic addition. It doesn't have to be difficult or scary, and it definitely doesn't require extensive training or expertise – it's really just another way of understanding music. The reason solfa is especially useful for preschool teaching is because of how much work you will be doing with listening and memory.

I use movable *do* solfa with *la* based minor in my studio and find it to be the perfect complement to letter-based note names. Singing in solfa helps students understand the relationship between notes in a scale and provides a gateway for even our youngest students to understanding transposition and harmony.

The simplest first exercise to help you find your feet with solfa in your preschool lessons is to sing simple two-note patterns with your students, starting with *so-mi*.

You can then move to *do-la*, which is the same interval of a minor 3rd, and switch back and forth between the two.

sing with me   do   la   do do la   do do do   la la la

Practise these two patterns multiple times. From here you can start to bring in *do-re-mi* patterns and, in time, the full pentatonic scale, *do-re-mi-so-la*. Just take it one step at a time and never introduce more than one new interval at a time (minor 2nd, major 3rd, etc.) so that your students can get really fluent and comfortable with the feeling of these movements through their voices.

The Curwen hand signs can be a great addition to these exercises and can help students to follow your lead more easily.

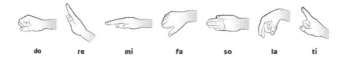

do   **re**   **mi**   **fa**   **so**   **la**   **ti**

Again, though, if you're new to solfa work or singing in general, take baby steps. Instead of the Curwen hand signs you can simply raise or lower your hand to demonstrate the pitch. You can also create your own little system, such as:

- Hands in the air for *la*
- Hands on head for *so*
- Hands on shoulders for *mi*
- Hands on hips for *re*
- Touch floor for *do*

The reason the Curwen hand signs are useful and popular with many teachers is that they are repeatable movements that show the notes of the scale. Whether you use these or improvise your own system, the important thing is to use some movement in order to engage more parts of your students' brains and help them follow along.

When your students become more proficient in solfa you can start to "translate" folk songs into solfa and use this to help them play the songs by ear and transpose them on the piano. You can then also use solfa to explore simple harmonisation:

- Find the I and the V, *do* and *so* for major songs and *la* and *mi* for minor songs.
- Play one bar of the melody at a time and ask your student to try the I and then the V. Which do they think fits better?
- Work through the song in this way and you will have created a simple duet accompaniment. It can also function as a left hand pattern if they're ready to play hands together.

Solfa can be a wonderful tool for your preschool lessons. Just take it bit by bit and don't feel you need to turn into a full solfa or Kodály studio in order to use this tool effectively. A little goes a long way.

SINGING AS A MEMORY AID

There's a reason we sing the alphabet to the tune of *Twinkle, Twinkle, Little Star.* Children learning a new language will often learn a translated *Head, Shoulders, Knees and Toes* and some kids can recite an impressive amount of the periodic table of the elements using *The Element Song*. When we employ songs or rhythmic chants we can learn things much more easily. This tactic is useful for all ages, but, when you don't have the advantage of being able to read words or notation to remind yourself, it can be the difference between retaining the information and not, or practising and not.

We can use songs to help our students remember musical concepts in the same way school teachers use them in the classroom. We have the added bonus of being able to use these songs to further reinforce pitch, rhythm and pulse by moving to them, as well as using the lyrics to help young students remember terms and concepts.

For example, a member of the *Vibrant Music Teaching* community created this modified version of the alphabet song which she kindly shared with me and other members. The tune is that of *Twinkle, Twinkle, Little Star* but the modified words go as follows:

A-B-C-D-E-F-G,
(march forward, one step per letter)
These are my piano keys.
(pretend to play keyboard)
Sometimes UP,
(reach arms high above head)
Sometimes DOWN,
(touch the floor)

My alphabet goes round and round!
(spin!)
G-F-E-D-C-B-A,
(march backward, one step per letter)
Let's play the piano way!
(pretend to play keyboard)

Songs like this are another great way to get playful, and this one always gives my students a giggle, especially when it comes to walking backwards.

Singing is also a fantastic help when you're working on rote pieces and you need students to be able to practise them at home. By singing these pieces (making up your own lyrics if the piece doesn't have any) over and over, students will be able to self-correct when playing them on their own.

Chapter 10
LISTENING

"Never miss a good chance to shut up."
Will Rogers

Some houses are *bursting* with music. **Some are not.**
By the time they're five years old, a child might have
heard thousands upon thousands of pieces of music,
ranging from classical to rock to jazz, or they may
have only heard music on the radio in public spaces
and ads on TV.

Think about this for a moment. When planning our
preschool lessons I think we need to be cognizant of
this disparity.

If you're here, reading this book, it's quite likely you
grew up in a musically rich household. Most teachers
I know had parents who loved a wide variety of music,
discussed it with them and danced around the house
to it. Many of us were even taken to live concerts
from a young age and got to see great performers in
action.

As music teachers, we need to provide opportunities
for and develop the skills of active listening. After all,
music is meant to be listened to. Developing great
listening skills with our young students is a big step
towards levelling the playing field for the kids who
come from less musically rich households.

You don't necessarily need to follow a curriculum or book to start to awaken your students' ears. Simply listening together and asking questions can do a great deal. But what questions should you ask?

LISTENING FOR TIMBRE

I don't remember the exact age I was (I would guess eight or nine), but I remember the moment when I realised my peers couldn't pick out different instruments in a recording. The conversation came to a pretty swift halt once I figured out that they weren't hearing what I was hearing. They couldn't tell the difference between the flutes and violins, and they didn't even seem to know what a bassoon was.

I'm not saying every child has to be able to recite every instrument of the orchestra and draw a labelled diagram of each...but having an awareness of the sounds different instruments make can inform how they listen to and play music down the line.

To encourage your students to listen for timbre start by listening to solo pieces together and asking them about what they hear. How does it sound different to the other instruments they've heard before? Show them pictures of the instrument as you listen and try miming playing along too, e.g. playing "air violin" or "air drums".

You can also make use of great pieces like *Peter and the Wolf* and *The Young Person's Guide to the Orchestra* to explore listening for timbre together.

LISTENING FOR PITCH

One of the basic ideas that preschoolers need to get used to is the difference between high and low sounds. They need to be able to find these on the piano, but also to distinguish them aurally too.

Explore this concept through movement by playing examples on the piano and having your student answer by stretching up to the sky if it's a high sound and crouching down on the floor if it's a low sound.

Always ask your students about the high and low sounds when listening to music as well to give them more practice with this important, but sometimes confusing, distinction.

LISTENING FOR DYNAMICS

Preschoolers can often confuse high vs low with soft vs loud. Therefore, you should work to include plenty of examples that are high and loud or low and soft when you're working on this skill.

As well as asking your student about the dynamics when listening to music, you can also work on this distinction through movement. Make sure to pick actions that are markedly different from the ones you are using for high and low sounds, such as holding your hands up as a lion's mane for loud sounds and as little mouse paws for soft sounds.

One advantage of spending time discussing dynamics

in music with your preschool students is that, by experiencing the effect dynamics have on the story and impact of music early on in their studies, they will learn how valuable they are. This means they're more likely to grow up to be young pianists who value dynamic markings. And I know we'd all love to spend a little less time telling our students to pay attention to the dynamics!

LISTENING FOR TEMPO

It's best to combine discussions about tempo with moving to the pulse of the music in order to get the best value for your lesson time. Make a habit of always asking whether a piece is fast or slow before and after you've tapped, marched or clapped along with it.

The Carnival of the Animals is a wonderful resource for exploring pitch, dynamics and tempo with your students. Talking about what makes each piece sound like the animal it represents can open up many conversations about these elements of music. It's also a great opportunity to get playful and move around the room as each animal as you listen!

Chapter 11
CREATING

"Creativity is contagious. Pass it on."
Albert Einstein

Creativity and play go hand in hand. If we only play the music of others, that's like learning to read language but never writing your own sentences, or reciting poems but never having a conversation. What a strange use of language that would be.

When students create their own music, whether improvised or composed, they go beyond the surface level and into the depths of real understanding. They can move things around, mix them up, play with the elements, and develop knowledge that can be applied flexibly later on and is not limited to one specific application.

CREATING IN THE MOMENT

Improvisation can be simple. You don't need to have jazz training to get started. And your students don't have to be producing beautiful music in every improvisation session in order for it to be valuable.

I see improvisation as a fantastic learning tool. It's a way for students to experience concepts without lengthy explanations and without having to have a complete understanding of the *why* behind what they're doing. That can come later.

I believe improvisation should start in the very first lesson. In fact, for most of my students it's the first thing they ever do on my piano. For preschoolers, I recommend sticking to duet improvisations so that you can support them with a great accompaniment.

If you need some tips to get you started, try creating music together on the black keys. You can play any simple chord progression in G flat, such as I–V–vi–IV, while your preschool student creates their own music using only black keys. Repeat the chord pattern as many times as you like followed by a very clear ending with a ritenuto and perfect cadence. Getting in the habit of giving a clear cadence like this at the end means that your student will start to sense when the ending is coming and you can begin to communicate through your improvisation.

You can use this same format to explore any scale, as well as other concepts too, such as different intervals and rhythm patterns. When you feel like you want a more comprehensive strategy for putting improvisation to use in your studio you can find it in the *Mini Musicians* and *Tiny Finger Takeoff* courses.

What if your preschool student doesn't seem to "get" this improvisation thing? What if they just bash away at the keys or are too nervous to play at all?

The former is more common so let's look at that first. If, when you say, "let's make some music together on the black keys!", your student does her best impression of a walrus playing the piano, please do not get discouraged or decide improvisation is just not for her. Some kids need to test out the different sounds and get used to the feeling of the keys in the beginning. If this means a few lessons where they are not playing anything that sounds remotely like music, that's A-OK. They just need to get it out of their system.

One extra parameter you should add to your instructions for students with this tendency, however, is to only play with one finger at a time. Don't correct them after they have given their walrus performance, though; wait until the following week, adjust your directions, and demonstrate how they can hop from key to key with one finger. Of course, once you have given clear instructions, feel free to correct your student if they're still playing clusters of keys at once. But don't worry or fuss too much if their playing is still quite random and not very melodic.

Trust me: the "music" will come in time. Just keep at it.

For the students who are nervous of improvisation and reluctant to play anything at all, the best thing to do is to keep narrowing the options down. This might seem counterintuitive but it's easier to be creative within clear boundaries, and these students may need stronger fences in order to feel secure that they won't *get it wrong*. Play your accompaniment part and show them very simple examples of what they might play, e.g. G flat–A flat–B flat or D flat–D flat–E flat. Most students will copy what you do at first but after several examples like this they will notice how easy it is to play something that sounds good and they'll start to explore a bit more.

Again, if they don't, do *not* give up. It doesn't mean that they're not creative or that improvisation isn't their thing. These tools are for everyone. Some just need a bit more breathing room and a bit more time to feel confident.

CREATING THEIR OWN PIECES

Just because a student isn't reading traditional notation yet doesn't mean they can't compose and notate their own pieces. Kris, for instance, believes in encouraging all students to try their hand at composition: "Why should they think that the only music they can play is what somebody buys in the store and gives to them one day?" Getting students involved in creating their own music helps them to see how music works from the inside out. Students (of any age) who compose are more appreciative of the details in the music they read because they understand what goes into it and they know that the decisions the composer made have been carefully thought out.

Preschool students who are not yet reading on the staff obviously do not need to notate their pieces on the staff either. Start with the music they are playing and have them compose within that system. For example, if they are reading using colour, they can compose using crayons. If they are using finger numbers, they can write a sequence of numbers to remember their song.

Even if you are not using any form of reading with your preschool students I would still suggest you incorporate composing into your lessons, as it can be a great first introduction to the idea that music can be written down in some way to help us remember it. Since you have no framework to start from you can use this as an opportunity to get extra creative. Ask your student what they could draw to help them remember their piece. You might be surprised what students will come up with using pictures, shapes or symbols.

PART 3

Outside the lessons

We spend less than 1% of our waking hours in a week with each student or group of students. What happens outside of the lessons is a big factor in determining how well our students progress.

When we apply this logic solely to practice we can end up banging our heads against the wall and feeling helpless when our students just will not practise...but, as a teacher, what you do in between lessons counts too. If I could go back in time to when I first started teaching, look myself in the eye and give one piece of advice it would be this: "Stop expecting magic and start planning for it." Back then, I was so concerned with what ought to be done in a lesson and with how things were supposed to go, but I wasn't actually putting up the scaffolding required.

I was telling parents that the kids should be practising, and telling the kids themselves what to practise, but I wasn't telling them how, and I wasn't helping them to establish a routine that made this possible. If you asked me whether I recommended that my students perform I would have said "absolutely!" – but I wasn't providing opportunities for them to do so in a supportive environment.

And the biggest mistake of all: I wasn't really planning my lessons. I had a rough sense of where I wanted students to go but, for the most part, I was a turn-the-page-teacher, following the books wherever they wanted to take us. That's just not good enough and it simply will not work with preschoolers.

In this section, we'll look at everything we do outside of our lesson time and how we can prepare students for success during the other 99% of the week.

Chapter 12
PRACTISING

"No one can teach riding so well as a horse."
C. S. Lewis

We all know how important practice is. I don't need to prattle on about that here. However, when you're teaching preschoolers you need to make some new decisions about your practice expectations. Don't assume preschoolers will practise in the same way as the rest of your studio. They're at a completely different stage and may need a different approach.

In the 'Forgetting' chapter, we wiped the slate clean and re-thought our lesson structure. Now it's time to do the same with practice.

PRACTISING...OR NOT?

There's actually an argument to be made for completely removing practice from the equation for your preschool students. Shock! Horror!

But I want you to at least consider it. In my *Mini Musicians* group lessons, I don't ask for any practice at all in the first year. I encourage parents to listen to music at home with their child, chat about it with them, and let them experiment with instruments... but there are no assignments. Nothing is required outside of the lesson. That's because the program is designed to be a great first introduction to piano concepts and a weekly musical experience.

This is perfect for many parents. Not everyone wants to become a daily practice coach. Some families want some form of music education for their children from a young age but they're in no rush to check off boxes and progress markers just yet. Their primary reason for having their child take piano lessons is to expose them to music and give them a love of it, and a once-a-week experience can do that.

On the other hand, if you want your students to make as much progress as possible you will need regular practice. And to do that you need the parents on board.

PRACTISING WITH A HELPING HAND

Parents are essential to successful practice for pre-school students. After all, many of these kiddos aren't even brushing their teeth yet without a reminder, so how can they be expected to practise without help? For maximum progress, we need to get parents to step into the role of practice coach.

So many of the issues and misunderstandings teachers have with parents over practice come from a lack of clear communication on the teacher's part and could easily be avoided.

Don't assume parents understand *anything* about practice. Really nothing.

Start from the basis that they don't know:

- That their child needs to practise
- That they need a piano at home to do so
- That they have a role in their child's success

I regularly see comments online from teachers complaining about a parent who didn't know one or all of these fundamental facts. Believe me, I understand the frustration in these posts. But let's just take a minute to put ourselves in the parent's shoes and think about what this means.

A parent who doesn't know that their child needs a piano, needs to practise on it, and needs their help to do so, is probably one who didn't get the opportunity to study music themselves, and maybe they didn't have any friends who did either. But they still sought out music lessons for their child. They understood it was important. Perhaps they felt they missed out on something.

Then they join the bewildering environment of our studio and feel like they're constantly missing pieces of information because we assume everyone knows "the basics". Is that a good way to start off a relationship with a new piano parent, with them feeling confused and inadequate? Is that going to help them feel confident to help their child at home?

Don't rely on what you consider to be common sense. You're in too deep to be able to accurately judge what "common" is.

I recommend holding a meeting, interview or meet-and-greet with every new student before they start lessons. At this meeting you can get to know your new student a little, give them a tour of your studio space, and talk the parent through how your studio works. As part of this, you can explain what type of instrument they need, how often they should practise, and where they can check the assignments. You should also give them tips on establishing a practice routine at home and share what works well for other parents.

You may already be doing this for all your new students, but it's doubly important for preschoolers. The younger the child, the more important the parent to their success.

But don't stop there.

Many teachers do explain all of this in the beginning, but then that's it; they don't discuss practice with the parent again – until there's a problem, that is. Until they've reached breaking point because practice is not happening or because the parent still hasn't upgraded the home instrument.

You'll have a much better relationship with your piano parents, and will achieve better results, if you check in regularly. When we ask about how practice is going and offer tips and suggestions at almost every lesson, parents don't feel like they're being chastised or reprimanded. And, with this more positive environment, they're more likely to tell us when there is a problem so that we can help them to fix it.

You're not the practice police for them, and they're not the practice police for their child. You're their advisor and they're their child's coach.

PRACTISING ROUTINES

So what advice should we give these fledgling practice coaches about establishing a routine? When should their child practise and for how long?

Well, we all know that's a classic "piece of string" question, but I will give you some general guidelines to get you going. Just make sure to tweak this advice as you go to suit your community and your culture.

The first thing I emphasise to every new piano parent in my studio is routine. I tell them they should focus solely on routine for at least the first semester so that practice truly becomes a habit. This means that they don't need to complete all the assignments every day, and they don't need to worry too much about the quality of the practice – they just need to get their child to the piano every day.

Carina advises her piano parents to get their child practising as often as possible in short bursts of just a few minutes at a time: "I tell them daily would be perfect. Five times a week is wonderful. At this age the students have time and often they practise two or three times a day when they pass the piano in the living room."

Hang on a sec...don't I want my students to practise efficiently and effectively? Didn't I write *The Piano Practice Physician's Handbook* to help teachers with exactly that?

Yes, I did. But I advise saving the practice strategies for the second semester and beyond. If your student is practising regularly as a matter of course, you can tweak and adjust their practice techniques later. If your student is not practising, you can talk about what they should be doing until you're blue in the face and they still won't be doing anything.

The most reliable way for a family to bring piano practice into their routine is to tie it to another activity in their day. Doing practice straight after lunch or while their dad makes dinner or their sister does her homework is much more effective because these things happen every day. Therefore, you should discourage your piano parents from simply linking practice to a time of day. Whether the time is vague (in the early afternoon) or specific (2pm), practice is more likely to get derailed because almost no family has the same routine every day of the week. Siblings will have sports or dance class, play dates will come up, and the unexpected will happen.

Check in on the routine regularly. Ask mum or dad about it every time you see them (or email them if you don't see them each week at the lesson) so that it becomes part of the weekly conversation and not an accusation. Remember: you're the coach's advisor, not the practice police.

PRACTISING INSTRUCTIONS

You may have gathered by now that most of your communication about practice will be with the parents, not the preschool student. Your assignment sheets or practice notebook should therefore be directed mostly towards the parents and give clear instructions that don't require musical experience to be understood. But it's also good to have picture-based elements that your student will be able to follow too.

For example, you can include characters for them to colour once they have completed their practice each day or boxes for them to tick off beside the various pieces they need to practise. You can also add stickers and drawings directly onto their books to help them remember what you worked on in the lesson.

These little touches are useful, not so much for enabling the preschooler to practise independently – they will still need their parents to organise the session, read directions and give reminders – but rather for allowing them to feel ownership over their practice. It's not something that is happening *to* them; it's a team effort and they're on the team.

As you will be working with many activities and pieces that are not written down, I highly recommend making use of videos to help your preschool students along outside the lesson. Many rote pieces come with reminder videos, and you can make your own for those that don't have them. Don't be intimidated if you don't feel tech-savvy. You can create a great video using any smartphone, upload it to YouTube for free, and send the link to your piano parents. It doesn't need to be fancy to be useful.

Chapter 13
PERFORMING

"If you're not nervous then you're not paying attention."
Miles Davis

Some teachers think that preschoolers are too young to be getting up and playing in front of an audience. However, the benefit of their starting to perform at such a young age is that they don't know they should be nervous. And if they have several performance experiences when they are too young to put much pressure on themselves, this lack of nerves tends to carry through into subsequent years too. Performing will feel normal to them, as if it's just what people do.

Having said that, I wouldn't recommend pushing a child (at any age) to perform if they don't want to. Invite them along to watch instead and they may feel comfortable enough to give it a go the next time.

PERFORMING IN RECITALS

Besides the lack of nerves, there's another fun bonus for preschoolers performing in concerts: the audience will love *whatever* they play! They're honestly just so teeny and adorable that people are delighted and impressed even if they just get up and play a single note.

So keep your recital repertoire choices simple when it comes to your preschool students. Pick out a piece they have been playing successfully in lessons (a duet is usually best) and have them show it off at the studio recital. Don't feel like you need a special show-stopping recital piece. A simple folk song or improvisation, played well, will always beat a fancier choice that overwhelms the kiddo.

If you are going to have your preschool student play in a studio recital, make sure to talk through what it will be like for several weeks leading up to the big day. Describe the audience, the hall, the clapping, the bowing, and everything else about the experience in detail and encourage the parents to do the same at home. Remember: a three-year-old has probably never even been to a concert and they don't have a frame of reference to enable them to imagine it for themselves.

PERFORMING IN MINI-CONCERTS

Another great option for preschool students is for them to do mini-concerts just for the family. When they have a few pieces ready you can invite their family into the lesson one week for the recital and have them play through the whole set. You can even have the student create their own program booklet and serve juice afterwards to make it more like a real recital.

This experience gives students something to work towards without too much pressure, and gives their families a chance to celebrate their achievements.

Chapter 14
PLANNING

"It does not do to leave a live dragon out of your calculations, if you live near him."
J.R.R. Tolkien

I'm aware that at this stage of the book your head might be close to exploding point. There is so much stuff to do in your preschool piano lessons and so many areas to cover! How on earth are we supposed to fit this all in? What's the best way to plan well balanced lessons?

Firstly, I'd just like to remind you of what we discussed in the 'Deciding' chapter about lesson length. I said you would end up wanting longer, not shorter, lessons once you saw all the activities we can do and concepts we can cover, and I wasn't wrong, was I? Make sure you set up your preschool piano lessons so that you do have enough time to cover everything, because there's no substitute for missing lesson time and no magic wand to wave to create more. Revisit that part of the 'Deciding' chapter if you need to.

Now let's talk about the nitty gritty of planning.

The first thing I recommend you do is make a list or mindmap of everything you want to include in a lesson and estimate roughly the amount of time each would take.

Below is an example of a mindmap for individual preschool lessons. (It would be similar for group classes, but the timings would work differently.)

Your mindmap may not look exactly like mine. You may have extra things you want to add or things you don't want to include, and you may want to give more or less time to certain elements. That's how it should be. The more "you" your plan is, the more confidence you'll have delivering it to students and communicating it to parents.

If you're having trouble coming up with activities, a good place to start is the table of contents in this book. You can always cross things out and add new things as you gain experience and your ideas develop. And if you want a ready-made curriculum you can find the *Mini Musicians* group program and the *Tiny Finger Takeoff* plans for one-on-one preschool lessons inside the *Vibrant Music Teaching* membership.

PLANNING A PREDICTABLE PATTERN

Once you have your list or map of the general categories you want to include, it's time to choose an order of activities that you will repeat each week. Making your pattern predictable is not only easier for you; it's also better for your students. Almost everything – the whole world – is still new information for 3–5-year-olds. So, although predictability may sound dull to us, it's essential for them.

Having the same format for every lesson allows your student to gradually get used to the pattern and flow of the lesson. This means that they'll be able to track the time better too, which means fewer questions about how long is left in the lesson.

Having visual and aural cues can also help your student follow where they are in the lesson. I use little picture symbols of the different aspects of the lesson. The pictures include a multicoloured piano to represent improvisation, a game counter for theory games, and a hand for technique work. I have a metal whiteboard in my studio so I put magnetic tape on the back of each little card and stick them up in order before the kids arrive. It's a simple system but it really helps with the flow of the lesson. (*Vibrant Music Teaching* members can find the 'Visual Lesson Plan Cards' in the library. If you're not a member you can get these cards as one of the bonuses that come with this book at: vibrantmusicteaching.com/play)

Whether it's a picture they look at or a song they listen out for, the more way markers a child has to help them follow your lesson structure, the less pushback you'll get when you move from one activity to the next.

There's no wrong way to structure your lessons, but here are some good rules of thumb:

- Don't plan to spend more than five minutes on any one activity
- Mix up on- and off-bench time, movement and stillness
- Start and finish with some easy student favourites that will make your student feel confident

But hang on...I've said not to spend more than five minutes on any one task and yet I've allocated 10 minutes for rote pieces in my mindmap. What gives?

While I don't recommend spending any more than five minutes (or possibly three minutes for particularly fidgety kiddos) on any one activity, I do recommend repeating things throughout your lesson. So my plan for all the activities in the mindmap might look like this:

1. Vocal warmups – 2 minutes
2. Stretches – 3 minutes
3. Posture – 2 minutes
4. Reading – 2 minutes
5. Rote – 3 minutes
6. Moving to the beat – 2 minutes
7. Listening – 3 minutes
8. Rote – 4 minutes
9. Improvising – 5 minutes
10. Singing folk songs – 5 minutes
11. Fingerplays – 2 minutes

12. Rote – 3 minutes
13. Reading – 3 minutes

I am absolutely *not* suggesting you set egg-timers and jump promptly from one activity to the next. But you'll probably be surprised how well this pacing works for your young student. It's much easier to keep them focused on the task at hand when you have a fast pace and loop back on concepts rather than doing a lot of repetitions in a row.

PLANNING TO REPEAT

Let's talk about that looping for a moment. You know how so much is new for a preschooler and how that can make them easily distracted and mean that they find it more difficult to track time? Well that very newness also has a fantastic upside for teachers: they don't mind repetition. In fact, preschoolers thrive on repetition – as long as it's not back to back.

Don't expect your little student to sit and play the same song five times in a row. Instead, come back to that song throughout the lesson and repeat it the following week...and two weeks after that...and a month after that. They will get something new out of that song each time they play it and they'll enjoy the feeling of competence they get from doing something they know they can be successful at. This holds true for movement activities, games and anything else you're working on. Your preschool student will find new layers of understanding each time, even when you feel like you've done it a thousand times before.

PLANNING FOR THE WIGGLES

Even with a plan that moves snappily from one activity to the next, you will occasionally hit a wall where a student just runs out of steam and can't focus on what you want them to focus on. When this happens, you have two options: move on to the next activity and either circle back to this one later in the lesson or the following week, or have a wiggle break.

Sometimes, all students need is to get up and wiggle for about 30 seconds in order to refocus and concentrate on the more challenging task again. Kris finds that the best approach is to factor wiggle time into the lesson: "You can't fight the wiggles. If they've got to wiggle, you've *gotta* wiggle."

I designed my *Silliness Siestas* for this very purpose (*Vibrant Music Teaching* members can grab these in the Printable Library) and you can make your own for your studio. Just write some fun and silly brain breaks on slips of paper and allow your student to pick one at random any time they need to get the wiggles out in order to focus. The tasks can be a mixture of dancing, miming and super silly movements, such as acting like a helicopter. (I keep mine in a polished coconut with a face for the extra playfulness factor.)

Whether you use *Silliness Siestas* or come up with your own solution, the most important thing is that you pay attention to the signs of wigglitis. Some kids will start to squirm and wriggle, others will get distracted by irrelevant objects in your room, and others still will try to chat with you or start to look sleepy. All kids need to move, no matter how "well-behaved" or how well they hide their wigglitis symptoms.

PLANNING TO THROW THE PLAN OUT THE WINDOW

Through my research for this book, and countless interactions with teachers from all over the world, I have come across the same theme again and again: great teachers plan their lessons thoroughly and have clear goals and strategies in place, but they are also prepared to completely scrap the plan at any time and they have a keen awareness of what the child in front of them needs in each moment.

All three of the teachers featured in this book said this in their own way:

"I'm a big planner but I'm not fixed on the plan. Many people have a problem with plans because they think they're fixed – but they are not. I don't care how long we need to get there and sometimes students need something in between." —Carina

"I think that, with these very young children, if you're fixated on your own agenda of ticking the boxes of a set curriculum – or not even a set curriculum but your own expectations – you're going to get anxious because these young children don't develop that way. You know they're not little robots that you can just plug in, program, and add the next level to when they need to be progressing." —Lyndel

"Teaching is being where they are and wanting what that teachable moment is going to be for them. And if they are enjoying and participating in one of the activities, I don't stop them just because there are three more activities I want to get to that day. That's not teaching...at least to me." —Kris

BALANCING

"A secret about juggling: Throwing is more important than catching. If you're good at throwing, the catching takes care of itself."
Seth Godin

I realise that at this stage your brain may feel weighed down with so many ideas and options to consider, and that the cogs might be struggling to turn with the sheer volume of information. That's why I want to leave you with some thoughts on a slightly fraught and overused, but nonetheless very important, subject: balance.

There are many seesaws and tightropes we need to navigate in our lives. As humans, we need to juggle possibilities with practicalities, new and shiny with tried and tested. As teachers, we need to orchestrate this delicate balancing act not just for ourselves but for our students too. We need to continue our education and be lifelong learners, as well as reserve time to actually absorb and put ideas into action.

And we need to plan lessons that keep this balance on a minute-to-minute, week-to-week and year-to-year basis.

When discussing this idea of balance with veteran preschool piano teachers one common theme always comes up, and it harkens back to the 'Forgetting' chapter: throw out your expectations of progress and follow the lead of the child sitting in front of you. This is a simple lesson, but it's one that we have to learn and relearn, again and again.

This doesn't mean not teaching, or following the child wherever they go no matter how irrelevant. But it does mean casting off your adult agenda and comparing the child only to themselves. Are they moving in the right direction? If so, it doesn't matter if they're not moving according to some outside measure of progress or in accordance with a curriculum. Children already get their fair share of box ticking and percentage marks in the school system, and piano, especially at the preschool level, should be a respite from that.

I hope that this book has given you practical information and ideas for your preschool piano lessons so that you and your youngest students can sing, move, listen and play together. But having activities and strategies is only the beginning. Now it's time for you to get to work and find the right balance for you.

Balance comes in when we put on our music teacher hats and consider all the many different aspects of

musicianship that we want our students to understand and gain skills in.

Imagine an old-fashioned scale, the kind with bowls
on either side...except this set of scales has far more
than two arms coming from the fulcrum point. Depending on your philosophies and priorities, you
may have a scale with 4, 6, 8 or even 10 arms.

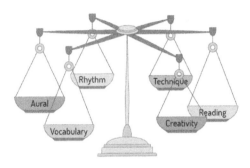

That's a lot to keep under control, but with an older
student it's just about manageable because they're
more predictable. The younger your student is, the
more likely they are to have off-days when they miss
a nap or get the wrong snack after their playgroup,
and on these occasions you may have to work in
ways you didn't plan for. Sometimes a child needs to
absorb a concept through dance or manipulatives or
rhymes, and it won't be the same every time for the
same child either.

This comes back to the importance of play. These
detours don't mean your preschool student isn't
learning. They're just doing it their way and at their
pace. When you put the kiddo firmly at the centre

of your scales and keep coming back to meet them where they are, you can't go far wrong.

Working with preschool-aged students also means we have more time to rebalance the scales when they get misaligned. There's no rush to get to reading or learn a certain word or develop finger strength because they've potentially got years of lessons ahead of them. We have the luxury of time. So let's use it to have fun, play and make music together.

Acknowledgements

I would like to thank Lyndel Kennedy, Kris Skaletski and Carina Busch for agreeing to share with me their experiences of teaching preschoolers as I prepared to write this book. It was wonderful to get perspectives from three different parts of the world (Australia, USA and Germany) so I could compare the differences and find the common threads that great preschool piano teachers share.

Thanks also to all of my own preschool students, from the first ever up to present day. Without my personal guinea pigs, giggling their way through my experiments, I wouldn't be the teacher I am today. Anyone who is having trouble finding the courage they need to try something new should look to a preschooler. They will inspire you with their willingness to explore and their determination to keep going when things are unfamiliar.

My own courage to start teaching preschoolers came from the online piano teaching community. If it weren't for the generous teachers who share posts, write articles and record videos, I never would have taken the leap.

And my determination to write this book might have wavered without the work of my wonderful proofreader, Janine Levine. Her attention to detail and passion for the art of language makes it a pleasure to discuss commas, hyphens and hyperlinks.

More from Nicola Cantan

Thank you for reading *Playful Preschool Piano Teaching*. If you liked the book, please leave a review wherever you purchased it. I'd truly appreciate it. And if you're interested in more resources like this, you might also like these.

VIBRANT MUSIC TEACHING MEMBERSHIP

Vibrant Music Teaching is the perfect resource to help you level-up your teaching and teach using more creativity. There is a library of video courses and every printable game and activity you could need for your students.

To get more information and sign up for membership, go to: www.vibrantmusicteaching/join

THE PIANO PRACTICE PHYSICIAN'S HAND-BOOK

We all know a huge amount of the learning that needs to occur happens in the practice room, not the lesson room. This book (specifically for piano teachers, although many of the ideas can be adapted) will help you to help your students practise more effectively. You can get it on Amazon or your favourite online or in-person bookshop.

RHYTHM IN 5

 Many piano students struggle with rhythm, but as teachers it's hard to fit in extra rhythm work, and even harder to make it fun. Rhythm in 5 will help you do that with movement and improvisation. You can get it on Amazon or your favourite online or in-person bookshop.

THINKING THEORY BOOKS

 *Thinking Theory* is a series of music theory workbooks designed to accelerate learning while providing plenty of reinforcement of each concept. All concepts are presented in a clear and concise way and page layouts are clean and consistent. No topic is introduced without being revisited several times later in the book. The workbooks incorporate solfa singing, rhythm work and carefully levelled theory concepts.

Take a look, at: thinkingtheorybooks.com

COLOURFUL KEYS BLOG

 Nicola writes regular articles and shares ideas on her blog, *Colourful Keys*. Check it out if you're looking for more piano teaching inspiration, at: www.colourfulkeys.com

Made in United States
North Haven, CT
31 May 2024

53130046R00075